Ailia

(What it's like to be 11 years old

and have Down syndrome)

By

Ailia Bliss Colin

Copyright Notices

Published under the Copyright Laws of the Library Of Congress Of The United States of America, by:

Bliss Publishing
3127 176th St.
Lansing, IL 60438

International Standard Book Number (ISBN) 978-0-9910996-1-0

Ailia

"A child should always say what's true,

And speak when he is spoken to,

And behave mannerly at table

At least as far as he is able."

Robert Louis Stevenson

I'm so proud of you, Ailia.

Love, Grandma Bliss

Introduction

"Ailia has to do a science project for school," Ailia's mother said.

"A science project? What are you going to do? Ailia likes science, but what kind of project can she research and present to her class?" These were her grandmother's questions.

It was her mother who came up with this idea. Ailia and Down syndrome would be the subject. Well, why not? This has been a topic for study within the family since the day Ailia was born. After talking with Ailia to see if it was okay, research was begun. What was the best way to explain Down syndrome to Ailia and then to her fourth grade class? What else did Ailia want to share with her class? Her project, with more support from Miss Lara, Ailia's aide, was a success. Her grandmother decided to put her presentation in book form.

Ailia

Hi, my name is Ailia. I live with my dad, mom, and two younger sisters. I'm eleven years old and I have Down syndrome. I'm writing about . . . Me!

I'm writing about what I know about Down syndrome and what it feels like to be an eleven year old girl who has Down syndrome.

Sometimes Down syndrome is called Trisomy 21. My biology is a little different from yours. This is a chromosome:

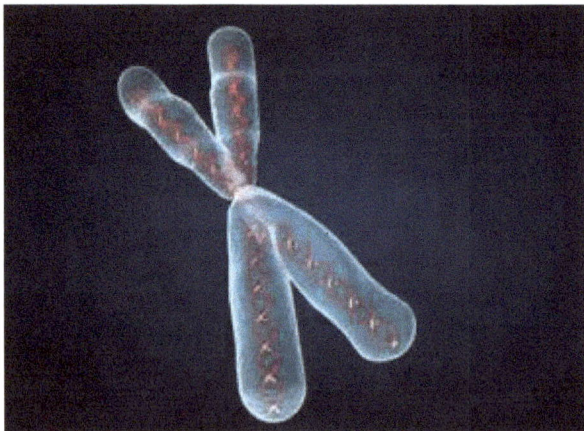

Chromosomes are made up of genes and a protein called chromatin. Chromosomes help determine things like what color your hair will be, what color your eyes will be, or how tall you will grow. They also are what make you a boy or a girl.

Most people have 23 pairs of chromosomes, for a total of 46 chromosomes, but I have 47. I was born with an extra copy of chromosome 21.

Biologists graph chromosomes like this:

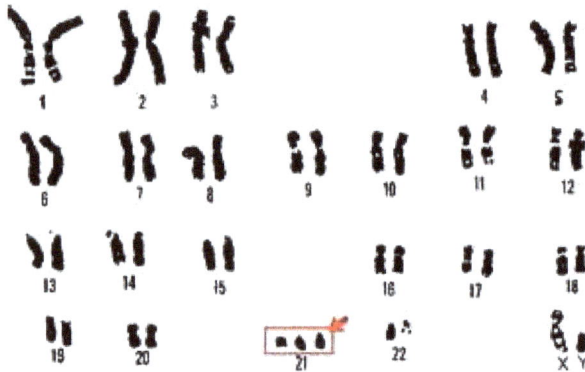

See how there are 3 bars at number 21?

That means this person has Trisomy 21,

just like me.

This one extra chromosome makes

some things harder for me to do. My

muscles are weaker, and it takes me a

little longer to learn things.

Nothing could stop me from sitting in on this yoga class!

Because the muscles in my mouth are weak, I have to work hard to speak clearly. Because my muscles are weak, I need to work a lot harder to walk, to climb, and to use my hands. But, I am much more like you than I am different.

I have thoughts and feelings, just like any other kid.

I love to listen to music and dance. My favorite songs are "Let It Go," "Gangnum Style," and "Krank."

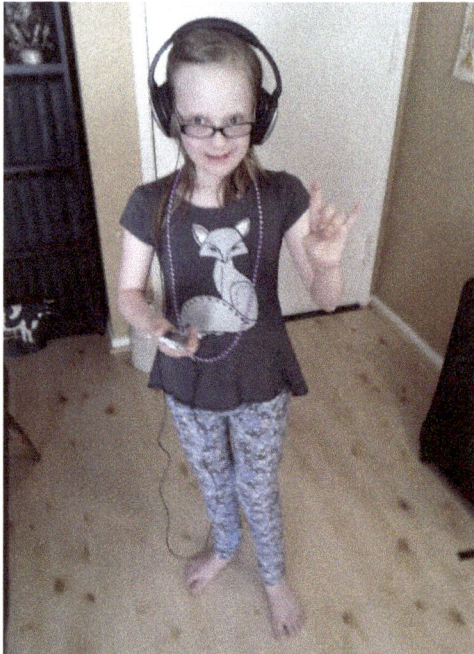

Wanna Dance?

I like to watch movies and hockey. My favorite TV show is Scooby Doo. I love pizza, broccoli, and cake. I also love big parties and I really love parades.

Here I am with my sister, Emily, and Bailey, the LA King's mascot. THAT was a FUN day!

Sometimes I talk to myself. I think about things out loud. Don't you do that sometimes? Have you seen people talk to their computers or shout at other people when they're driving in a car?

I'm glad my sister Emily is just PRETENDING to drive!

I like slightly off-kilter jokes. I get them. Sometimes people say things that strike me funny and I'm off in the corner laughing to myself.

My dad can always make me laugh!

"I can walk like an Egyptian!"

I don't like a lot of loud noises. I don't like it when my little sister has my grandma read "The Tortoise and the Hare" five times and then there's no time to read my book.

I look a little different here…because
I'm dressed as a ladybug!

Sometimes people avoid me because I look a little different or because I am hard to understand. That's too bad because I could be a good friend.

My parents are teaching me to "treat others with respect." It's what I want for me. I guess it's also what you want for you.

Like you, I have hopes and dreams of the future. I am learning to cook. I want to cook for you someday.

My school helps me. My speech therapist helps me speak clearer. My physical therapist helps me run better. My occupational therapist is helping me write better. My glasses help me see more clearly.

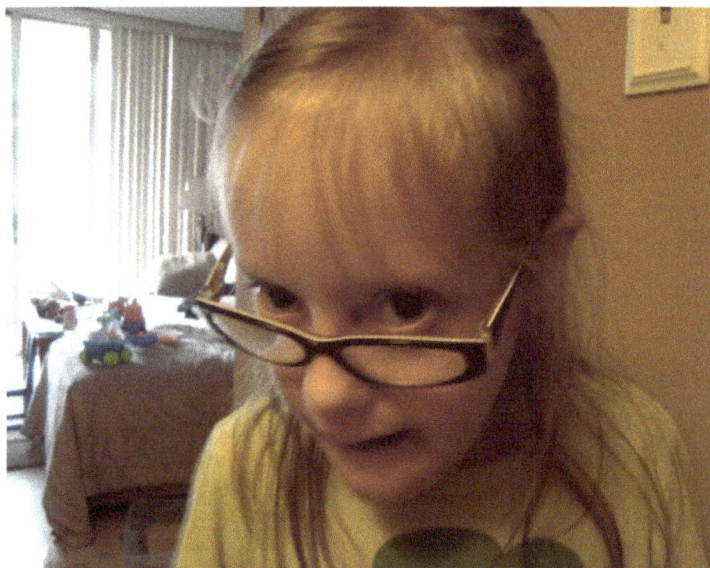

Not all people born with Down syndrome are the same. Some have heart problems. Some can't eat certain foods. Some have very bad eyesight or problems with their ears.

But, a lot of people without Trisomy 21 have these problems too. It is all a matter of the chromosomes. This is a picture of double helix molecules and chromosomes:

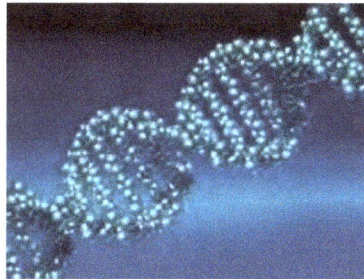

My chromosomes have made me who I am, just like your chromosomes

have made you who you are. We are all

unique.

   And that is the way it should be.

I was reading to my grandmother and

she said I was doing well. In fact, she

said that I was a "wonderment."

Grandma Bliss encourages me!

Grandma Bliss realized I knew and could understand a lot of words that I had trouble pronouncing. I told her, "That's right. Slow and steady wins the race."

I'm forever blowing bubbles

My name is Ailia. It is spelled the same backward and forward. Either way, it's just me, Ailia.

About the Author

Ailia is an eleven year old girl with Down syndrome. She is in the fourth grade and spends part of her day in a special education class and part of her day in a mainstream class. She also takes speech therapy, physical therapy and occupational therapy. Her days are busy.

This story developed out of a science assignment for her mainstream class, in which Ailia spoke about Down syndrome and what it means to her. She lives in Glendale, California with her parents and two younger sisters.

Ailia and her sisters, Ivy and Emily

Acknowledgements

I want to thank my mother and my father, Cindy and Mike Colin, for helping me with my science project. I want to thank my dad for helping me pronounce "chromosome."

Thank you, Grandma Bliss, for reading stories to me.

I also want to thank Miss Lara Kaloghlian for helping me every day at school. You have made so much possible for me.

I want to thank Grandma's friend, Pam Osbourne, for her wise counsel and her help in putting this book together. I also want to thank another friend, Jari Franklin, for her many helpful suggestions.

Another thank you goes to Grandpa Arthur Woods for his quiet expressions of love and support. Thank you also to Sue and Chuck Colin and Jana and Bill Stelter for always being there for me.

Psssssssst….it's just me, Ailia!

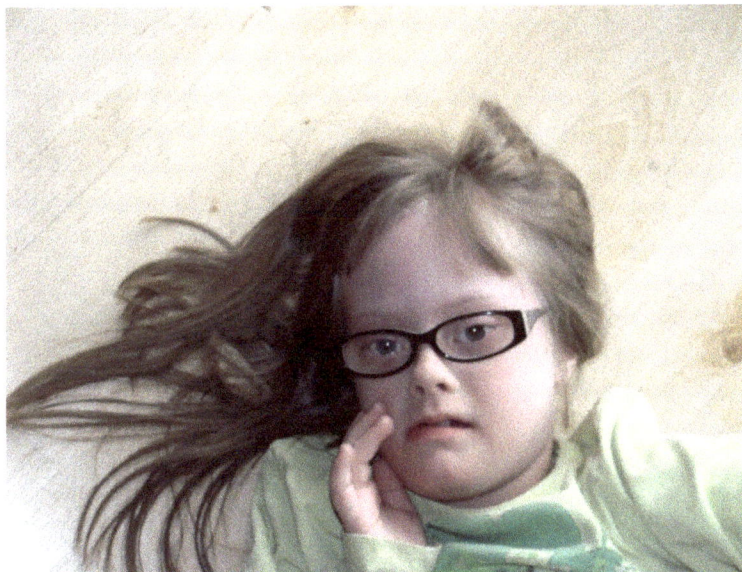

www.ingramcontent.com/pod-product-compliance
Lightning Source LLC
Chambersburg PA
CBHW041928040426
42443CB00018B/3498